Letter Carriers

BY CECILIA MINDEN

Content Adviser:
Tim Wakefield, President,
Postalmag.com,
Mesquite, Texas

Published in the United States of America by The Child's World®
PO Box 326
Chanhassen, MN 55317-0326
800-599-READ
www.childsworld.com

Acknowledgements

The Child's World®: Mary Berendes, Publishing Director

Editorial Directions, Inc.: E. Russell Primm, Editorial Director; Katie Marsico, Managing Editor and
Line Editor; Judith Shiffer, Assistant Editor; Caroline Wood, Editorial Assistant; Susan Hindman,
Copy Editor; Wendy Mead, Proofreader; Mike Helenthal, Rory Mabin, and Caroline Wood, Fact
Checkers; Tim Griffin/IndexServ, Indexer; Cian Loughlin O'Day, Photo Researcher; Linda S. Koutris,
Photo Selector

The Design Lab: Kathleen Petelinsek, Design and Art Production

Photographs ©: Cover: left—Creatas, right/frontispiece—Hemera Technologies.
Interior: 4, 10, 25, 27—Photodisc/Getty Images; 5—RubberBall Productions; 7—Denis Scott/Cor-
bis; 8-9—LWA/Dann Tardiff/Corbis; 11—Peter Arnold, Inc./Alamy Images; 12-13, 19—Claudia
Walpole; 14-15—Tony Arruza/Corbis; 17—Kim Karpeles/Alamy Images; 20—Bob Pardue/Alamy
Images; 22-23—David R. Frazier Photolibrary, Inc./Alamy Images; 24—Bruce Herman/Stone/Getty
Images; 26—Cathrine Wessel/Corbis; 29—Kathleen Petelinsek.

Library of Congress Cataloging-in-Publication Data

Minden, Cecilia.
  Letter carriers / by Cecilia Minden.
     p. cm. — (Neighborhood helpers)
  Includes bibliographical references and index.
  ISBN 1-59296-568-7 (library bound : alk. paper)
  1. Letter carriers—Juvenile literature. 2. Occupations—Juvenile literature. [1. Letter carriers.
2. Occupations.] I. Title. II. Series.
  HE6241.M56 2006
  383'.145—dc22   2005026212

TABLE OF CONTENTS

Max

Hello. My name is Max. Many people live and work in my neighborhood. Each of them helps the neighborhood in different ways.

I thought of all the things I like to do. I like to be outside. I like to take long walks in my neighborhood. I have a good memory for names and faces.

How could I help my neighborhood when I grow up?

When Did This Job Start?

Benjamin Franklin became postmaster of Philadelphia, Pennsylvania, in 1737. His job was to make mail delivery better. Franklin was named postmaster general for all the colonies in 1753. He had a mail wagon travel each week between Philadelphia and Boston, Massachusetts. Franklin traveled 1,600 miles (2,600 kilometers) to review each of the post offices along the way.

I COULD BE A LETTER CARRIER!

Letter carriers get to be outside much of the day. They know everybody in the neighborhood.

Best of all, letter carriers make people happy when they deliver cards and letters from family and friends.

Letter carriers get to know everyone in the neighborhood by delivering the mail.

Where Can I Learn More?

National Association
of Letter Carriers
100 Indiana Avenue NW
Washington, DC
20001-2144

U.S. Postal Service
Headquarters
Personnel Division
475 L'Enfant Plaza SW
Room 1813
Washington, DC
20260-4261

LEARN ABOUT THIS NEIGHBORHOOD HELPER!

The best way to learn is to ask questions. Words such as *who, what, where, when,* and *why* will help me learn about being a letter carrier.

Asking your letter carrier questions will help you learn more about his job.

WHO CAN BECOME A LETTER CARRIER?

Boys and girls who have good memories may want to become letter carriers. Letter carriers also need to be friendly and enjoy working with the public.

Letter carriers are important neighborhood helpers. They bring cards, letters, packages, and magazines to people's front doors.

Letter carriers must always be friendly when dealing with the public.

MEET A LETTER CARRIER!

This is Peter Walpole. Peter has been a letter carrier for eighteen years. He works in Charlottesville, Virginia. When Peter is not delivering the mail, he likes to spend time with his family, write stories, and play golf.

Peter has worked as a letter carrier since 1987.

How Many Letter Carriers Are There?

About 334,000 people work as letter carriers.

WHERE CAN I LEARN TO BE A LETTER CARRIER?

People who want to be letter carriers need to get a high score on a special test given by the United States Postal Service. Having a good memory will help you get a high score!

New letter carriers get training from other workers before they start delivering the mail. They learn how to organize the mail and where to deliver it.

New letter carriers usually train with more experienced workers.

How Much School Will I Need?

Letter carriers must have a high school diploma. They also must pass a written test and take a physical exam.

Mail bag

Mail cart

Mail truck

parcels (PAR-suhlz) packages

WHAT DOES A LETTER CARRIER NEED TO DO HIS JOB?

Peter drives a postal truck made just for delivering mail. Inside his truck are places to put bundles of letters and **parcels.**

The first thing Peter does when he goes to work is check his truck to make sure the lights and engine are working. He won't be able to deliver the mail if his truck doesn't work!

Peter also has to know special words that letter carriers use to describe

Letter carriers have to check their trucks to make sure everything is working properly.

their work. For example, Peter uses big rubber bands to hold the letters together. This is called "strapping out" the mail. Knowing these special words makes it easier for Peter to communicate with other letter carriers.

What Clothes Will I Wear?

Comfortable walking shoes

Postal uniform

Some letter carriers walk to deliver the mail. These carriers are outside in all sorts of weather— sometimes very hot, sometimes very cold. Other letter carriers drive a car or truck.

route (ROWT) a path or course that is mapped out

WHERE DOES A LETTER CARRIER WORK?

Peter works at a post office. He goes to work early in the morning when most people are still asleep. He then begins sorting mail into the proper delivery order for his **route.** Next he loads the mail and packages for that day into his truck.

Peter delivers the mail to each stop along his route, until lunchtime.

Peter follows a mail route when he works.

UNITED STATES
POSTAL SERVICE

Then he takes a break for about half an hour. Peter delivers the mail along the rest of his route after lunch. He also picks up mail that has been dropped in mailboxes.

Peter delivers the mail to his last stop and then drives back to the post office. He puts the mail he has picked up in a big hamper for **postal clerks** to sort.

Some letter carriers are also responsible for picking up mail that people drop in mailboxes.

postal clerks (POS-tuhl KLERKS) postal workers who sort through and organize mail

WHO WORKS WITH LETTER CARRIERS?

The U.S. Postal Service is a very large operation. Clerks and mail handlers bring Peter the mail for his route each day. There are also truck drivers, airplane pilots, and special police officers called postal inspectors. Maintenance crews care for the postal trucks, buildings, and equipment and make sure everything is working properly. These people work together every day to make sure the mail gets delivered.

Clerks and mail handlers help sort the mail for letter carriers.

What Other Jobs Might I Like?

Courier and messenger

Meter reader

Postal clerk

Subway operator

WHEN DOES A LETTER CARRIER HAVE TO BE EXTRA CAREFUL?

Did you know Dog Bite Prevention Week is in May? The U.S. Postal Service reports more than 3,000 dog bites each year. Most dogs on a letter carrier's route are friendly, but workers need to know how to avoid animals that are not friendly.

Letter carriers sometimes face unfriendly animals along their route.

How Might My Job Change

Letter carriers get more experience and eventually get better routes. Some letter carriers move into jobs where they are in charge of other letter carriers.

Is This Job Growing?

The need for letter carriers will not grow.

I WANT TO BE A LETTER CARRIER!

I think being a letter carrier would be a great way to be a neighborhood helper. Someday I may be the person you see delivering mail in your neighborhood!

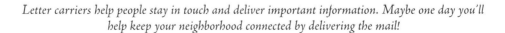

Letter carriers help people stay in touch and deliver important information. Maybe one day you'll help keep your neighborhood connected by delivering the mail!

WHY DON'T YOU TRY BEING A LETTER CARRIER?

Do you think you would like to be a letter carrier?
You need to know how to check an envelope to
make sure it includes all the right information.
Look at the envelope on the right and answer these
questions:

+ Is the writing clear and easy to read?
+ Does the address include the name and street
  address?
+ Does the address include the city, state, and
  zip code?

+ Is there a return address in the upper left-hand corner?
+ Is there enough postage on this letter?

Do you think a letter carrier would deliver this letter?

Jane Doe
630 W. Iron St.
Butte, MT 59701-2346

Mr. Smith
3541 16th St. NW
Washington, DC 20010-3041

Letter carriers need to be sure envelopes have all the right information.

HOW TO LEARN MORE ABOUT LETTER CARRIERS

BOOKS

Flanagan, Alice, and Christine Osinski (photographer). *Here Comes Mr. Eventoff with the Mail!* Danbury, Conn.: Children's Press, 1998.

Klingel, Cynthia, and Robert B. Noyed. *Postal Workers.* Chanhassen, Minn.: The Child's World, 2002.

Knudsen, Shannon. *Postal Workers.* Minneapolis: Lerner Publications, 2006.

Kottke, Jan. *A Day with a Mail Carrier.* Danbury, Conn.: Children's Press, 2000.

WEB SITES

Visit our home page for lots of links about letter carriers:

http://www.childsworld.com/links

Note to Parents, Teachers, and Librarians:

We routinely check our Web links to make sure they're safe, active sites—so encourage your readers to check them out!

ABOUT THE AUTHOR:

Dr. Cecilia Minden is a university professor and reading specialist with classroom and administrative experience in grades K–12. She is the author of many books for early readers. Cecilia and her husband Dave Cupp live in North Carolina. She earned her PhD in reading education from the University of Virginia.

INDEX